AN IDEAS INTO ACTION GUIDEBOOK

Interpersonal Savvy

Building and Maintaining Solid Working Relationships

IDEAS INTO ACTION GUIDEBOOKS

Aimed at managers and executives who are concerned with their own and others' development, each guidebook in this series gives specific advice on how to complete a developmental task or solve a leadership problem.

CONTRIBUTORS	Bill Gentry, Kelly Hannum, Ancella Livers, Hughes Van Stichel, Meena Wilson, Sophia Zhao
DIRECTOR OF ASSESSMENTS, TOOLS, AND PUBLICATIONS	Sylvester Taylor
MANAGER, PUBLICATION DEVELOPMENT	Peter Scisco
EDITORS	Stephen Rush Karen Lewis
ASSOCIATE EDITOR	Shaun Martin
COPY EDITOR	Tazmen Hansen
WRITER	Taylor Scisco
DESIGN AND LAYOUT	Joanne Ferguson
COVER DESIGN	Laura J. Gibson Chris Wilson, 29 & Company
RIGHTS AND PERMISSIONS	Kelly Lombardino

Copyright ©2013 Center for Creative Leadership.

All Rights Reserved. No part of this publication may be reproduced, stored in a retrieval system, or transmitted, in any form or by any means, electronic, mechanical, photocopying, recording, or otherwise, without the prior written permission of the publisher. Printed in the United States of America.

CCL No. 455
ISBN No. 978-1-60491-156-5

CENTER FOR CREATIVE LEADERSHIP
POST OFFICE BOX 26300
GREENSBORO, NORTH CAROLINA 27438-6300
336-288-7210
WWW.CCL.ORG / PUBLICATIONS

Interpersonal Savvy

Building and Maintaining Solid Working Relationships

Center for
Creative
Leadership

www.ccl.org

THE IDEAS INTO ACTION GUIDEBOOK SERIES

This series of guidebooks draws on the practical knowledge that the Center for Creative Leadership (CCL) has generated since its inception in 1970. The purpose of the series is to provide leaders with specific advice on how to complete a developmental task or solve a leadership challenge. In doing that, the series carries out CCL's mission to advance the understanding, practice, and development of leadership for the benefit of society worldwide.

CCL's unique position as a research and education organization supports a community of accomplished scholars and educators in a community of shared knowledge. CCL's knowledge community holds certain principles in common, and its members work together to understand and generate practical responses to the ever-changing circumstances of leadership and organizational challenges.

In its interactions with a richly varied client population, in its research into the effect of leadership on organizational performance and sustainability, and in its deep insight into the workings of organizations, CCL creates new, sound ideas that leaders all over the world put into action every day. We believe you will find the Ideas Into Action Guidebooks an important addition to your leadership toolkit.

Table of Contents

7   What Is Interpersonal Savvy?

9   Interpersonal Savvy in the Workplace

11   How to Develop Interpersonal Savvy

19   Your Behaviors—Too Much of a Good Thing?

20   Red Flag Scenarios

24   Your Red Flag Journal and How to Use It

26   It's Not a Trick—It's Real Life

28   Background

29   Suggested Resources

IN BRIEF

Interpersonal savvy is the ability to build and maintain solid working relationships with your superiors, colleagues, and direct reports. It helps you make the most out of everyday interactions, using skills such as good listening, empathy, sincerity, and teamwork. Your behaviors shape how others perceive you in the workplace, and a firm knowledge of interpersonal savvy will allow you to best shape those perceptions to achieve the greatest results. Self-awareness of the positive qualities you want to demonstrate, combined with specific actions to implement those qualities, will lead to positive outcomes in how others view and interact with you. One thing to watch out for is taking a good quality too far—for example, letting your self-respect become arrogance. Being on the lookout for these scenarios and taking the time to implement more positive alternatives will further help to raise your interpersonal skills. By continuing to develop interpersonal savvy, whether you think you have the skills or not, you will become a more thoughtful, friendly, approachable, and trustworthy leader who can achieve results.

What Is Interpersonal Savvy?

Interpersonal savvy is your ability to build and maintain solid working relationships with colleagues, superiors, and direct reports. It's a capacity made up of several interlocking skills, such as the following:

- good listening
- empathy
- honesty
- sincerity
- a strong orientation toward teamwork
- trustworthiness
- supportiveness
- a willingness to share responsibility

We all like to believe we possess these qualities, and everyone does have the capacity for interpersonal savvy. The challenge is building that capacity so others see that you have these qualities. You must be a good listener, an honest person, sincere, and trustworthy. This is especially important as you transition into positions of greater authority, where more people will look to you for leadership.

Daily behaviors shape people's perceptions of you, and those perceptions determine their feelings about you. Interpersonal savvy allows you to better navigate and understand those perceptions and to build trust with your colleagues, which will in turn improve their (and your) efforts in the organization. This kind of open behavior toward others can be intimidating for you and your colleagues, which is why it's even more important that you exhibit such behavior. Your example shows colleagues that your workplace is a safe place to be patient, honest, and straightforward when communicating.

Throughout this guidebook, we use the terms *savvy*, *skills*, and *behaviors* somewhat interchangeably, though technically these words have different definitions. We view these terms as linked: developing your interpersonal skills will lead to tangible behaviors that you can exhibit in the workplace, and continually exhibiting such behaviors will lead to an increase in your overall interpersonal savvy. Therefore, rather than focusing on the three terms as separate, we view them as interrelated aspects of an overall framework of interpersonal savvy and, consequently, use these terms as such throughout the guidebook.

Also, this guidebook will discuss how to change your behaviors to improve others' perceptions of you, rather than focusing on changing any internal feelings or tendencies you may have. While a strong moral character is certainly important in succeeding as a leader, we seek a pragmatic approach by suggesting tangible, real-world skills you can implement to improve your interpersonal savvy. For instance, you may view yourself as shy and generally introverted, but implementing some of these interpersonal behaviors may result in others perceiving you as outgoing and a great communicator. This is not a deceptive tactic; if you exhibit positive interpersonal skills, others will perceive you as interpersonally savvy, regardless of whether you feel that you are. As stated above, perception is important, and we seek to help you develop skills that will provide real-world benefits in how you are viewed in the workplace.

Daily behaviors shape people's perceptions of you, and those perceptions determine their feelings about you.

Interpersonal Savvy in the Workplace

You already use the skills associated with interpersonal savvy when you make friends or meet new people. Outside work, these skills might seem effortless—less like a tool set and more like an aura of friendliness and approachability you radiate to other people. After all, outside work you can generally choose the people you see and talk to each day, and they have the same freedom, so you and the people around you tend to gravitate toward people you naturally like. It's not hard to be a good listener when you meet a famous athlete in the park downtown. He has great stories about different players he's worked with and great matches he's played, and you'll naturally use interpersonal savvy to keep talking to this stranger because you're interested in what he has to say.

The producer of a radio program realizes that the most recent episode of the program reported false information about a local amusement park. She has high standards of journalistic integrity and is very upset about the discovery. When she meets with her team after learning the news, she furiously demands to know who dropped the ball. Her attitude makes it clear that the consequences will be dire. If the producer were more inquiring, she might learn that the reporter cleared the story with the head of the park and presented it in good faith. But will the reporter speak up after the producer's outburst? Maybe not. What kind of example does this set for the other reporters? They learn that they have to be vigilant when fact-checking a story, but they may also feel less confident about proposing risky story ideas because of the producer's rash behavior. This will cost the producer in the long run by weakening the amount of trust and openness reporters have for her.

But what if your organization is in the middle of a broad-sweeping software rollout and the team you lead is running into problems with the new interface? In this kind of situation, it's tempting to forgo politeness and force your way to the point. What is the problem? What is the fix? Implement it. Next!

Interpersonal savvy, however, is much more than politeness. The reality is that your interpersonal savvy before the crisis occurs could affect the team's ability to communicate with you during a crisis like the hypothetical software rollout. Does your team perceive you as a trusting, available leader? If so, your team members may be happy to explain to you their concerns or problems with the new software and seek your advice in addressing those concerns. However, if they expect a terse or hostile response from you, or if they're worried about looking uninformed in front of you, they may keep their problems to themselves and try to fix problems without your help or supervision. Maybe they'll do fine without needing to ask you any questions, but if your team members don't feel that you value them and their perceptions, you'll be the last to know if something goes wrong.

Often, good interpersonal skills privilege patience over expediency. You may have to wait for the best results to appear. Hasty, impatient behavior can wreck positive relationships even as it grants short-term results. Nobody wants to feel like an expendable resource, and if your direct reports or your coworkers feel that way around you, expect them to avoid you.

If you have used positive interpersonal skills with your team in the time leading up to the software update, you might anticipate what kinds of problems the team could run into. Which members of your team like to run a simple routine each day? Which ones crave new tasks and don't like to do one thing over and over for hours? Who has the most trouble remembering passwords? If you have effective relationships with your team members, you'll be able to answer these questions.

Interpersonal savvy is a two-way street. Maintaining these kinds of relationships with colleagues means they will know better how to communicate with you. When a colleague tries to explain why she thinks her system keeps crashing, she'll know how best to express herself to help you understand, and she'll be able to anticipate when you might make a hasty judgment without complete information. When you find yourself in such a situation, you'll feel the difference.

How to Develop Interpersonal Savvy

At times, the practice of effective interpersonal savvy can feel vague and ill defined. You may be wondering whether there is a way to achieve reliable results in your relationships by following a set formula. Simply put, no; people are not mathematical figures. There is no way to perfectly track the return on your interpersonal investment. You may not be able to plot your results on a chart, but you can still be pragmatic in your approach. Think of these behaviors as a skill set providing you with the tools you need to inspire confidence in your team and respect for your leadership.

Goals for Developing Interpersonal Savvy

What are your interpersonal goals? How do you want others to perceive you? If you could choose an ideal image of yourself and project that image to others, what qualities would it have? Once you've set goals for yourself, it may be easier than you think to apply the appropriate skills. Take a look at the following skills to determine whether implementing them will help develop your interpersonal savvy.

I want to be a leader who shares responsibility. Fostering this perception in others can empower members of your team

Worksheet 1: Perception and Interpersonal Savvy

Consider how others perceive you in the workplace, particularly in how you interact and communicate with others. You may want to ask trusted colleagues to give you candid, honest answers to these questions.

List two of the positive ways others perceive you in the workplace.

For those two positive perceptions, list behaviors that you believe contribute to those perceptions.

List two of the negative ways others perceive you in the workplace.

For those two negative perceptions, list behaviors that you believe contribute to those perceptions.

because it builds trust between you and them, builds their confidence in their own talents, and helps them invest personally in projects. All these results help you achieve your goals. If you want to project this quality, try these behaviors.

Assign high-visibility tasks to other team members when appropriate. Nobody likes to toil in obscurity. Give people the opportunity to prove themselves! If it turns out well, you might find other people coming to you asking for a similar chance. If it doesn't turn out well, it becomes an opportunity to learn for both of you.

Share relevant information when delegating duties, and make sure everyone understands that information. People need a broad understanding of their tasks in order to do their best work—this includes understanding specifics about expectations, resources, processes, and so forth. Foster transparency in making assignments, and you may be surprised by the new ideas that come your way.

Take the time to learn the skills and desires of direct reports. Use what you learn to find assignments that take advantage of their skills and help them achieve their goals. Matching tasks to skill sets helps efficiency, and it may help people see you as a caring leader who values individual abilities. You will also learn what kinds of assignments will comfortably stretch your direct reports so that they can develop further.

I want to be a leader who promotes trustworthiness. Letting people know that you trust them is a great way to motivate them and gain their loyalty. By demonstrating trust in others, you allow them to feel secure around you, which may make them more confident about sharing ideas and concerns with you. Try these behaviors to generate trust.

Find sincere ways to talk positively about individuals both to them and to others. Everyone has strengths and at least one outstanding skill. Make a habit of identifying those strengths, and don't keep them to yourself. You might surprise others with a positive observation about how they demonstrate advanced organizational skills or a determined attitude to get results. Recognizing and speaking about those kinds of behaviors can really change the way people identify with the team. They will go out of their way to prove you right and will trust you to represent them to others.

Guard information that was given to you in confidence. You don't have to share sensitive information to act upon it. If Stacy tells you she's overwhelmed with a demanding workload, you don't have to mention her by name when you make the case for hiring more talent. By holding information in confidence, you gain the trust of your coworkers and may increase their openness in the future.

Share your feelings and experiences and encourage others to do the same. Remember to be sincere, and don't worry about being inspirational all the time. This is a chance to show a little vulnerability in order to create a safe environment among your coworkers. Such an environment results in free-flowing information, which will let you make better decisions that apply more immediately to your team's needs.

I want to be a leader who is open and available. When people see you as a welcoming presence at work, it reduces stress and lets colleagues know you are on their side. To project such a quality, try these behaviors.

Establish an open-door policy so that people feel comfortable coming into your office. When you wall yourself off from others, they may see you as an adversary instead of an ally. You should strive to make your office more like a public marketplace—a forum where people are welcome to share ideas, create solutions, speak their minds, ask for help, or simply make a quick connection.

Stop to engage in hallway conversations. Sharing a few words in an informal setting takes a little bit of the pressure off during work and lets people know you're interested in their thoughts. People will feel more relaxed around you if you're not afraid to let your guard down and if you join in their conversations.

I want to be a leader with good listening skills. Once you've established that you're a trustworthy, available leader, people will want to talk to you. This is good. When people approach you to share information or just to talk casually, you get to know your team better. Do people seem stressed out, or are they relaxed? Do they seem excited about their current projects or bored and hoping for a change? Are they eager for new opportunities? To get the most out of these conversations, practice good listening skills and using the following behaviors.

Nod your head and keep eye contact with the person speaking. Simple visual cues like these let people know you're interested in what they have to say.

Ask clarifying questions, such as "Can you help me understand what you mean by that?" Some people become nervous when they try to explain something to their boss, and if you can take the burden of understanding onto yourself, it lightens the burden of expression from the speaker.

Rephrase others' statements to confirm your understanding. Rephrasing increases the efficiency of your communication by lowering the chances of misunderstanding. It's an easy way to make sure you and your colleagues are on the same page.

Once you've established that you're a trustworthy, available leader, people will want to talk to you. This is good.

I want to be a leader who is sympathetic. The skills described in the previous section are well suited to situations when a colleague engages you in a conversation that's all about work and the tasks at hand. But what if someone comes into your office feeling overwhelmed, upset, or just desperate to blow off steam? Work isn't easy all the time, even for a competent team, and work-related stress and concerns can affect people's performance. When colleagues really trust you, they might come to you for help in such matters. In that kind of situation, it's important to show sympathy by using the following behaviors.

Avoid offering advice or judgment unless asked. This can be difficult, but it's important to remember that simply talking about problems can help people work out the issues for themselves. Don't worry about whether you are helpful or come up with a solution. More often than not, your presence and attention can be all another person needs.

Relate the other individual's situation to your own life, but don't assume you know exactly what he or she is experiencing. If a coworker's troubles sound familiar to you, don't keep it to yourself. Sometimes this is just what a person needs to hear. Sharing your own experience will let your coworker feel trusted. Just be careful not to place your experience above the other person's. After all, you don't want colleagues to walk away from the conversation worried about you or, worse, feeling that you've invalidated their problem.

Restate what the other person says to you or acknowledge some of the feelings he or she is experiencing. Let your coworker know his or her feelings are valid before you respond. This is also a good way to make sure you understand what the other person is telling you. Restating something a colleague says lets that person hear and clarify his or her position or give you more information based on what you say.

Sharing your own experience will let your coworker feel trusted. Just be careful not to place your experience above the other person's.

Assessment 1: Your Positive Interpersonal Behaviors

Reflect on how often you exhibit the following behaviors in your interactions with others. Circle the best answer.

I share responsibility with my team members and my direct reports.

    Always   Very Often   Sometimes   Not Often   Never

I trust others to complete their tasks and responsibilities.

    Always   Very Often   Sometimes   Not Often   Never

I listen to the opinions and ideas of others.

    Always   Very Often   Sometimes   Not Often   Never

I show empathy toward others when they bring me their problems.

    Always   Very Often   Sometimes   Not Often   Never

If you scored yourself low on any of the above behaviors, consider what behaviors you could implement to help improve that area. For instance, if you scored low in trusting others to complete their tasks and responsibilities, you may be micromanaging and need to give your direct reports more freedom and support to complete their tasks. If you scored low on sharing responsibility, you might want to think about projects you can share with others in order to complete the tasks sooner or more effectively.

Furthermore, if you're having trouble assessing your interpersonal savvy, consider using a 360-degree assessment. These assessments allow you to obtain opinions on your performance from peers, direct reports, your boss, senior staff, and even individuals outside your organization, such as customers. When combined, these opinions provide a comprehensive assessment of your performance and may help you obtain a better understanding of how others perceive your interpersonal savvy.

The Importance of Camaraderie

You can use the behaviors described in Assessment 1 to build a sense of camaraderie within your team. Camaraderie is intangible and hard to measure, but invaluable when a difficult situation arises. Say demand suddenly spikes for the watches your company manufactures, and your team of customer service reps receives double the usual workload. A team with a strong sense of camaraderie will come together to face the challenge head-on, not simply because it's work and it has to get done, but because each person knows his or her help is needed across the team.

Without this sense of camaraderie, individuals will feel disconnected from their teammates and uninterested in the work of others. They may pass responsibility down the line, doing the minimum amount of work to shift tasks off their desks. This can lead to bottlenecks in the work flow or hurt feelings. In such a workplace, individuals are not interested in doing their best since they have no confidence that work will be appreciated.

Assessment 2: Camaraderie

Think about a time when your team suffered from a lack of camaraderie in the face of a critical challenge.

- What was the challenge that the team faced? Was there anything different about this challenge from the challenges with which it normally dealt?

- What did the lack of camaraderie look like? For instance, consider interactions between team members or the overall progress of the project.

- What did the team do in response to the challenge? Was its effort successful? What did success look like?

- What could you have done that might have improved the team's sense of camaraderie? If you did take action, what did you do and what was the result?

Your Behaviors—Too Much of a Good Thing?

Just as positive behaviors can help you build interpersonal savvy and project the qualities you want, faulty behaviors can damage those projections and lead to interpersonal incompetence. Some of these behaviors may help you get ahead in the short term, making you stand out from your peers by delivering fast results, but you'll find yourself hitting a point of diminishing returns. If you treat people as resources, you will eventually expend them.

Some of these negative interpersonal habits are illustrated on reality TV, where so-called experts are shown getting angry and yelling at people with very little provocation or using unjustifiably harsh language that makes normal rudeness seem friendly by comparison. Such shows

> **If you treat people as resources, you will eventually expend them.**

present this behavior as no-nonsense expertise, but TV leaders have the luxury of changing their staff for every episode (or season) of the show, so they have fresh relationships to burn. Most leaders do not have that luxury and must treat their team members less like fuel and more like a garden or pasture—a renewable resource that takes care and tending to foster.

Be vigilant for some of the following faulty interpersonal behaviors.

When Pride and Self-Respect Become Arrogance

People are drawn to leaders who have a healthy pride in their work and a sense of self-respect, but arrogance makes people suspicious and stops them from rooting for you. Do you look away while others are speaking? Do you drum your fingers on your desk or tap a pencil during conversations? When you disagree with an idea, do you say things like "That's ridiculous!" in an absolute tone, cutting off the conversation before it can move forward? People may consider you arrogant if you do this kind of thing too often. You might unintentionally create a situation in which members of your own team would take satisfaction from your failure. That's not healthy for anybody.

When Direct Communication Becomes Insensitivity

Do you cut people off while they are speaking and not apologize for it afterward? Do you call people ignorant? Do you make private information public, even when it's given to you in confidence? If you indulge in this behavior, people might think of you as insensitive. You can reach a point where frankness becomes rudeness, and rudeness won't help you get results faster or encourage team members to work harder. It's just unpleasant.

Red Flag Scenarios

You might be asking, "Why would I behave in any of these negative patterns when I've just read all about other positive behaviors I could use instead?" It seems like an easy fix—behave less negatively and more positively, right? Your intentions are on the right track, but putting them into practice isn't as easy as it might sound.

Faulty interpersonal behaviors don't just come out of nowhere. They are usually automatic or instinctive reactions to unfamiliar or frustrating situations. For instance, you're in charge of a magazine and it's getting close to press time. You have a fixed deadline, and it looks as if an important article in the month's issue isn't going to be finished in time. Maybe the author didn't finish it, or there's been a fact-checking error and you can't run the story. You call a meeting with the staff to discuss solutions, and somehow the meeting gets sidetracked into a discussion of the typefaces that'll be used on the cover this month. It might be your instinct in this situation to interrupt the discussion and say, "We're getting distracted. Who's a good writer who can produce a new article by Thursday? I need names and numbers!" While this response is totally valid and might even yield the results you want, it's still a short-term solution and it doesn't inspire a lot of confidence in your team. If some members of your team come to believe you think of their concerns as distractions, how likely are they to speak up in future meetings? Such a perception has the power to shape the way people feel about their work. You have the ability to make them feel valuable in this situation so that the next time team members face a challenge together, they'll have the confidence to speak up. Positive interpersonal behaviors are easy to implement when everything's going well, but when inconvenient or unexpected challenges arise, you may be tempted to discard those behaviors just when they're needed most.

This imaginary situation is an example of a red flag scenario. A red flag scenario makes faulty interpersonal behaviors feel more expedient. You might need results in a hurry and throw your weight around to get them. You might feel threatened or vulnerable, as if the stakes of the situation are too high. Since many positive interpersonal behaviors involve projecting a certain amount of vulnerability while remaining secure (for instance, directly giving feedback to a colleague, which could open you up to criticism unless you express your opinions in an appropriate and tactful way), remaining interpersonally competent when you are actually in a vulnerable situation can be difficult. Or you could be facing a challenge you've never faced before, and your inexperience could force you to depend on others for help. However, that same inexperience could lead you to micromanage and dominate those helping you, rather than trusting them to render the assistance you need.

The Domino Effect

Red flag scenarios often have negative feelings at their core. These negative feelings are the beginning of a domino effect that leads from feelings to thoughts to behaviors. This chain of events usually happens so fast that we don't even notice it. For example, you might be driving home from an errand when you notice you're starving and pull over at the nearest fast-food restaurant. That might seem like a snap decision, but in reality at least three things happen in this scenario. First, you *feel* hungry. Second, you *think*, "I want to eat something. Is there food nearby?" Third, you *behave* in a certain way by driving up to the first restaurant you see.

Now, technically, you've solved your problem. You've gotten food, and you aren't feeling hungry anymore. But what if you'd slowed down this domino effect right when it started? You might have been able to transform your feeling of hunger into a more productive thought, which would have led to a more personally valuable behavior. After all, if the first thing you'd thought of when you noticed you were hungry was the zucchini and teriyaki sauce in your refrigerator at home, you might be eating some home-cooked stir-fry rather than fast food. It'd be less expensive and better for your body. This is a very small-scale example, but you can apply this rewiring of the feeling-thought-behavior reaction at work.

In the magazine deadline example mentioned previously, the problem of the missing article seems simple and linear. The only way to solve the problem, from your point of view, is to get another article on file as quickly as possible. You want to know who's a good writer who can deliver something printable on a tight schedule, and you want to know now! When the meeting swerves off topic, you feel frustrated and impatient. This feeling leads you to think, "I'm fed up with all this talk about typefaces. Whose meeting is this anyway?" This leads to your behavior of clearing your throat loudly and saying to those present, "We're getting distracted. Who's a good writer who can produce a new article by Thursday? I need names and numbers!" Without stopping to analyze your feeling-thought-behavior chain, you've acted in a manner that could damage your interpersonal relationships with the rest of your team.

How to Detect Red Flag Scenarios

What if you'd trained yourself to detect a red flag scenario like this even as it happens? When you begin to feel frustrated and impatient, you'll notice your own feelings right away, and you'll have foresight into the kind of behavior you're likely to exhibit in such a scenario. You can rewire your own reaction because you've already subverted the second stage of the reaction by thinking to yourself, "I'm in a red flag scenario. This is an opportunity to use my interpersonal savvy." Now you can use the proper tools for the situation. Consider the previous example. You could say something like "I think the cover is important, of course. Is there a time later in the day we could talk about that? Right now, I'm really worried about the missing article. Does anyone have any suggestions on that subject?" Now you've validated the concerns of particular team members and committed to helping them, shared your own feelings with the team, and facilitated a conversation with them, rather than narrowing that conversation to a single possibility. As a result, you learn that another article you're planning to run could probably be rewritten with more depth to make up the empty space left by the lost article. At the same time, you're likely to get recommendations for writers who can help you out in the way you'd originally envisioned. Now you have two solutions to your problem instead of one!

We've contrived this scenario somewhat to illustrate the usefulness of interpersonal savvy. But even if things hadn't worked out so smoothly, would anything have been lost by using positive interpersonal behaviors rather than an impatient gut reaction? You risk nothing by behaving in this way, and you stand to gain improved relationships and better solutions.

Your Red Flag Journal and How to Use It

The key to transforming a frustrating red flag scenario into an opportunity for interpersonal savvy is recognizing the scenario and your own feelings about it. One way you can learn to slow down the feeling-thought-behavior chain of events is by keeping a journal of various conversations you have throughout your day. Try to pick out conversations or situations that make you feel pressured, uncomfortable, impatient, angry, or bored. This is your chance to take control of those situations and make them work for you.

After you've logged a few of these conversations or situations, look over them and see whether you can pick out any patterns. Are there similarities between any of these situations? Can any of them be avoided in the future, or can you expect to encounter them again as a normal part of your work life? Is there a particular coworker whose name appears often in your journal? Perhaps that person isn't interpersonally savvy and you can use him or her as a model for what not to do. Of course, you can't just use your journal as an excuse to ignore or dismiss the person. Instead, use it to reexamine your own interpersonal savvy to see how to best interact with the person.

The most important thing to identify in your journal entries is the feeling you experienced during a particular situation. Even if you didn't write down a specific name for a feeling, like *impatient*, *bored*, or *overwhelmed*, you can use your writing to relive the situation and identify your feelings. These feelings at the root of your behavior are what you need to assess and adjust.

Worksheet 2: Red Flag Journal

Use this journal to gather information about your red flags and behaviors. Afterward, reflect on what you have written to help you become more aware of such flags in the future.

Specific Encounter or Situation
What caused you to react in an incompetent manner? Be specific when describing the other person's behavior or the situation.

Feelings
What did you feel when you encountered this situation?

Thoughts
What did you think in response to those feelings?

Behaviors
How did you behave in response to your feelings and thoughts?

What You Can Do Differently in the Future
How could you have acted differently? For instance, what point in the feeling-thought-behavior chain could you tweak in order to produce better results in the future?

Studying your journal will strengthen your ability to identify similar situations in the future. The next time a challenge arises, you'll recognize it and think, "Wait! This looks familiar . . . ." When that happens, you've already taken control of the feeling-thought-behavior chain. Now you can decide how to act rather than simply acting on your gut. You can choose to be interpersonally savvy.

It's Not a Trick—It's Real Life

Perhaps this entire discussion about building interpersonal savvy comes across to you as a little too simple. "After all," you might be thinking, "isn't this just a kind of trick? Is it really good to project personal attributes I don't actually possess?" The short answer is that you have nothing to worry about in that regard. You have the capacity for interpersonal savvy because you're a human being, and we use skills like these all the time in our personal lives to comfort sick family members, delight our friends with old stories, or teach a stranger how to play chess. Good leaders use these skills in both their personal and professional lives, helping foster and improve relationships with colleagues as well as friends. You can use this guidebook to train yourself for that very task. By utilizing positive interpersonal behaviors, you won't be tricking people into believing you have natural empathy or a sincere desire to understand the needs of others. You'll be revealing those qualities in yourself.

It's natural to be nervous about making these sorts of changes. At first, you may feel exposed by the principles of availability, honesty, and sympathy that ground positive interpersonal behavior. You might feel phony the first time you invite people out for barbecue or ask someone down the hall about a new movie. But just because you are deliberately practicing these behaviors doesn't

Worksheet 3: Assess, Challenge, and Support

Answer the following questions (based on CCL's assessment, challenge, and support model of development) to examine your interpersonal savvy. In this model, participants receive *assessments* from others regarding their performance in a specific area and gain a wider picture of the current status of their development. They then find a *challenge* that pushes them out of their comfort zone and encourages personal and professional development through adversity. They also develop a strategy to help navigate this challenge, which builds their capacity to successfully overcome difficult situations. Finally, they obtain and receive *support* from supplementary materials, coworkers, additional training, and so forth.

What perceptions about your interpersonal savvy do you wish to change?

What specific behaviors can you identify that influence that perception about your interpersonal savvy?

Develop a strategy you can implement to help change this perception of your interpersonal savvy.

What sort of support will you get in order to maintain the change? List people and resources such as books and training.

mean you're faking it. You're just experimenting and giving yourself an opportunity to be surprised by and to learn from the results. Even if you have trouble with these habits at first, the more you practice, the more they will become a part of you. Eventually, you won't have to think about it at all. Instead of rewiring your gut reaction, you'll find that your first instinct is to speak as openly and invitingly as possible.

The results of this kind of behavior are very real. You can't graph them or put them in a presentation, but their effect will show in how your direct reports, your peers, and your boss react to you. Your interpersonal savvy can bring out the best work from your team because people are happy to help leaders who are friendly, trustworthy, and approachable. Let's say a friend of yours runs into problems and calls you for help. Even though you have lots of work to do, you're happy to help because of your relationship with your friend. That's what a good relationship allows—positive feelings in both good and challenging times. It's possible to create that kind of relationship with your colleagues too.

Background

CCL's extensive research into leadership and communication shows that effective leaders utilize successful communication skills as a way to improve morale, efficiency, and success in the workplace. While lower-level leaders are judged primarily by their actions and the results, upper-level managers are judged by both their actions and their relationships with others, further highlighting the need for interpersonal savvy. These findings are supported by CCL's work in workplace communication, including how to give effective feedback, as well as communicating across cultural boundaries. All these areas require a solid understanding of interpersonal savvy in order to successfully facilitate communication.

CCL has also conducted extensive research into derailment: understanding why successful leaders end up stalling or negatively impacting their otherwise successful careers. In particular, executives cited problems with interpersonal relationships as one of the top reasons for derailment. With this in mind, CCL designed the feeling-thought-behavior model as a way for leaders to become mindful of how underlying personal factors can ultimately impact their interactions with others. CCL's assessment tool Benchmarks also provides a way for leaders to understand what areas of their leadership need improvement. It identifies strengths and development needs, encourages and guides change, and offers strategic insights for leaders to use to enhance and strengthen their leadership skills.

Suggested Resources

Goleman, D. (2007). *Social intelligence: The new science of human relationships*. New York, NY: Bantam Dell.

Grayson, C., & Baldwin, D. (2007). *Leadership networking: Connect, collaborate, create*. Greensboro, NC: Center for Creative Leadership.

Hoppe, M. H. (2006). *Active listening: Improve your ability to listen and lead*. Greensboro, NC: Center for Creative Leadership.

Kirkland, K., & Manoogian, S. (1998). *Ongoing feedback: How to get it, how to use it*. Greensboro, NC: Center for Creative Leadership.

Lindoerfer, D. (2008). *Raising sensitive issues in a team*. Greensboro, NC: Center for Creative Leadership.

Prince, D. W., & Hoppe, M. H. (2000). *Communicating across cultures*. Greensboro, NC: Center for Creative Leadership.

Scharlatt, H. (2008). *Selling your ideas to your organization.* Greensboro, NC: Center for Creative Leadership.

Smith, R., & Campbell, M. (2011). *Talent conversations: What they are, why they're crucial, and how to do them right.* Greensboro, NC: Center for Creative Leadership.

Weitzel, S. R. (2000). *Feedback that works: How to build and deliver your message.* Greensboro, NC: Center for Creative Leadership.

Ordering Information

TO GET MORE INFORMATION, TO ORDER OTHER IDEAS INTO ACTION GUIDEBOOKS, OR TO FIND OUT ABOUT BULK-ORDER DISCOUNTS, PLEASE CONTACT US BY PHONE AT 336-545-2810 OR VISIT OUR ONLINE BOOKSTORE AT WWW.CCL.ORG/GUIDEBOOKS.

CCL's Ideas Into Action Guidebooks

are short, quick, easy references

for employees and practicing managers at all levels, and are a wonderful addition to your personal development toolbox. You'll receive information on teams, coaching, feedback, conflict, innovation, career success, resiliency, and more. Use our volume discounts to benefit your entire organization, or take advantage of our packages for teams, feedback, individual leadership development, and conflict. Or buy the entire set of competencies in the Comprehensive Guidebook Set!

To learn more and order, visit **www.ccl.org/guidebooks.**

Join myCCL PREMIUM Today!

Premium members of CCL's online leadership community receive a 25% discount on all CCL Press publications. Learn about this and many other benefits of myCCL PREMIUM membership at **www.ccl.org/mycclbenefits**.

Center for Creative Leadership

www.ccl.org